zion

Crab Orchard Series in Poetry
Open Competition Award

zion

POEMS BY TJ JARRETT

Crab Orchard Review &
Southern Illinois University Press
Carbondale

17 16 15 14   4 3 2 1

The Crab Orchard Series in Poetry is a joint publishing venture of
Southern Illinois University Press and *Crab Orchard Review*. This series has
been made possible by the generous support of the Office of the President
of Southern Illinois University and the Office of the Vice Chancellor for
Academic Affairs and Provost at Southern Illinois University Carbondale.

Editor of the Crab Orchard Series in Poetry: Jon Tribble
Judge for the 2013 Open Competition Award: Rodney Jones

Library of Congress Cataloging-in-Publication Data
Jarrett, TJ, 1973–
[Poems. Selections]
Zion / TJ Jarrett.
   pages cm. — (Crab Orchard series in poetry)
"Open Competition Award."
ISBN 978-0-8093-3356-1 (paperback)
ISBN 0-8093-3356-2 (paperback)
ISBN 978-0-8093-3357-8 (ebook)
ISBN 0-8093-3357-0 (ebook)
I. Title.
PS3610.A7725A6 2014
811'.6—dc23   2014001766

For Mary Laura Brown
(1919–2012)

By the rivers of Babylon, there we sat down and wept, when we remembered Zion.

—*Psalm 137:1*

Contents

one

My Grandmother Describes the Radiance

Dark Girl,

this body
has always been

more waiting room
than cage

At the Hospital

As she lay dying, we were left alone together
while she was swimming with the voices of the dead;

I dared not listen because she was never
talking to me. But then, she propped herself up

on an elbow and said to me: *I asked so much of her,*
so much of you and your mother and some would say

too much. And I just can't, I can't yet say I am sorry for it.
And she lay down again, drowning in that river.

Theodore Bilbo Attends My Sickbed

When the ache was just too much, I'd skip
down the hill to the slip where you
and a small boat were always waiting.

There, we would draw out the sloop
into the glassy-eyed river
and sit for hours in silence.

The fish would swim up to the hull,
coming up just short of the surface
then turning away again—

their white bellies barely visible
writing *surrender, surrender* on the water.

Maybe there never was any river. Maybe the only true thing is
that I would come back to the island, lift its lush grasses
and earth to myself and call it my body.

Maybe the only true thing is that you held
my lolling head between your hands and whispered:

I await our reckoning.

Meridian, MS 1978: Miss Polly Attends the Altar at Mt. Zion

I want to be moved, to forgive, to let forgiveness bear away
memory: you spitting in my face, saying *you are dead,*

dead. Nigger, you are dead. But already it is welling up in me,
this thing called forgiveness, and I reach up to your head

to bring you down, to make the metaphor apparent. You kneel.
You are on your knees now. You came for this. We let you come

into the house of the Lord for this. You have spread your arms
in a gesture of the Christ to say *forgive me. I come in peace.*

Forgive me.
                    And I want to be moved. For so long, I was stone.
For you, I was stone. Oh Lord, move me. I want to be moved.

The Body Sings to All Its Parts

Zora, Ethel, Mary, Mega, Dot, and I are gathered here
as if after war. We embrace and learn to love what is left

of our bodies. We reach to one another, touching, touching
the bodies we once knew whole. But we don't speak of that.

We have gathered. We have tea. We talk about the weather.
When we speak of weather, we speak of the bodies we saw

in the treetops and rooftops, their arms waving and waving
before they were subsumed. Necessarily, we are talking about

the dead. We are talking of this body's tempests—how quickly
it turns against itself. We are not impolite. We maintain silence

about the parts we had to surrender. We had only ourselves
and the body to blame. We may well wonder if our parts

long for a kind of reunion by and by. But we have doubts
and of those doubts, we could go on and on and on.

When They Say You Can't Go Home Again

No one tells you that the road is endless,
but you will not starve. The road is strewn with apples—

the trees no longer able to contain their fruit or beauty.
They will not tell you what you have called home

is unrecognizable—a jumble of fallen leaves, burning.
It is all consumed; it is we who consumed it, even its ember and ash.

Like I said, you will not starve. No one tells you
this nostalgia is a kind of poison or how long,

how long you must wander and despair.
They never report the bodies—

split from root to throat,
split from bloat and want.

Meridian, Last Night

Last night, I dreamt I went to Meridian again, and
in the dream, a slight dark girl darts from the side

of the house, arms waving, waving while a woman
inside resists the building's collapse on its own

emptiness. The house is still standing and in ruin.
As it always was. As always.

Of these things on earth I know:
I cannot return. There is no time,

even now, that was golden above another.
Every epoch has its trials. We are human.

We are failing. We are always falling down.
The past was always more menace than I'd imagined;

the past is both retribution and reward
now that it has been endured.

And it is right that we stand in its ruin,
among all this longing and decay.

How to Love the Country of Your Birth

Call it beloved. Call it
by each true name:

Appalachia of My Discontent.
Port of Forced Return.

Call it your shining
city on a hill. Upon finding

no natives to kill on your approach,
burn the niggers out. Build your city,

burn it down. Build your
city, burn it down. Exhaust

all metaphors for fire before
repenting. Speak, then, of the part

leading the whole to rot.
Will you stand long enough,

will you endure the night fire,
collect all that must be saved—

its embers cooling like a bullet
in your cupped hands?

Will you cleave the heart in half,
will you cradle your city there,

will you carry it?

Theodore Bilbo Begins His Confession

Now that we are both dead
I can tell you everything.

Sometimes, I would watch you
wading through the marshes

farther up into the cypress grove
but you would not take notice

of my gaze. You would dry yourself,
button up your dress, braid

your hair still wet with river water and
stare out into a distance, but I did not

know what it was you were thinking
in that quiet. I knew that there

were places I could still not enter,
a peace inside I could not reach

and I hated you for it, even more
than I hated myself for seeking

ways to conquer. Once, you brushed
my shirtsleeve as you were clearing

the dinner plates, and I felt a shiver
all inside as if I had wandered into

the house of the dead. I yelled at you
and you blinked back implacably.

I could not sleep after that.
I could not sleep.

two

How a Question Becomes a Lie

Riot in Memphis, May 1, 1866

Why must it
come to this?

Why do you
force my hand?

Will you take
the bullet or

will you choose
to burn?

Don't you see
what you made me do?

Must you go on
screaming?

Why do you make me
do this to you?
Why do you make me
do this to you?

Theodore Bilbo and I Reverse the Miracle

Any man could tell you that the
narrative of love requires an obstacle,

how natural it is to cast your burdens
on the waters of any inland sea

just to see what washes away, what remains.
Didn't you know a woman could drive a man

to scale a levee in the dark, use his own
hands to dig through until the water pours out

without regard to himself or consequence?

How easy it is to turn away,
leaving its detritus gasping on the shore.

He'd say: *there are rivers that can't be crossed.*
He'd say: *where none exist, a river must be made.*

Miss Polly Experiences the Consequences of Gravity

Eventually, the night reduces itself to parts, and the owl
is an owl. The tree is a tree. And things stop standing in

for other things. There is the night, and the night contains
the owl and the owl doesn't distinguish itself from that night

or the trees and moon therein. I am an interloper here.
I am human and I have come into a knowing of myself.

Here is the owl again. Here is the night. Here are the trees, the stars,
and something singing in the dark. And the owl moves its wings

against that night, aloft because one is not subject to powers
that cannot be named. I am a woman. I have come into knowing

anything you can name can fail you; nothing of the body
can be claimed. The owl is an owl. The night is a night.

To be free of metaphor is a mercy. Anything that can be named
can fail you. What you think you know is so far

from where we started. Fear nothing, but trust nothing you see.
Not the self, this body, those wings.

The Precipitating Event

In that time, God begat an inland sea
and when the water let out of the land

we gathered our bindles. Some traveled north,
others west, and we traveled east toward Queenstown

where we remained. But in the time we waited,
the water swallowed us and we learned all she held

within. I loved the river and she loved me.
In that time I learned the difference

between lumber and bone. She could hold
a body within for days, then thrust the whole

aloft in her current. What is containment
if not love? There is embrace, and a violence

in it. She called to us: *Do not leave me,*
but we thought this violent love

could not follow. We were wrong.
My God. My God.

Meridian, MS 1958: My Grandmother Meditates on the Miracles of the Christ

In the world we knew, what went blind stayed blind.
What was laid low, languished. The world we knew was dark

but manageable. The world we knew favored speed
or steel. Or both. We could run when they took up arms or

we could square the body against the pain we each would know.
The world revealed itself in this way, the choice it offered.

Hard then, to pray for more than this. But we did pray. Oh,
how we prayed. We prayed to the river to spare us flood. To the trees

and their turning. To the wind and its lamentation. If you know
nothing of prayer, know this: to pray is to ask—*Lord, will we be delivered?*

The world we knew said *no.* Said *wait.* Said *no* again. To pray is to ask—
Lord, have mercy. The world we knew said *no*, said *wait*, said *wait.*

And the Lord said unto us: *You ask not for My mercy; go forth
and ask your brethren.* And we were sore and right afraid.

1973: My Mother Cleaves Herself in Two

I am born. I dream the nightroom of your body,
and in that place, you sing, build me of words,

tell me the story of the locust: how she does not know
herself except in the presence of another. She will split

herself in two, shear the thorax, cast off the shell of herself
and consume what-she-was as afterbirth so that she may live.

Locusts reveal themselves one to another to yet another
like this, crowding the horizon—slick, black, gleaming

from prose to plague. You sing me there in your gloaming.
There, in your nighthouse, you knit me of words. I am born.

Your voice. It is sweet and filled with longing. I rise from the inside,
from the inside to the outside as if to say, *I hear you. I am listening.*

How We Arrived

First by boat, then by foot. Toward the inland, we carried you. And some carried the body, and others carried its words. It has always been thus. There is the body and there are its words, and they come together to assemble a man. When you have lost everything, the body sings to all its parts. *We are here,* the body says. *We are not yet dead. Here are the words of which we have been made.* Do not despair; you are never left with nothing. You would be amazed at how much a body wants to live. You can examine the contents of the soul, but the body has always had its own attentions. It is right the body has its way with us. And it is right this is as it has always been.

Meridian, MS 1951: Vice in Proper Form

There would be a hole in the earth where a town should be.
And we would be dead or low to the ground. Dark Girl,

if the world took proper shape: we would not be sheep; we were not
lambs led toward slaughter. Some would take the form of rodent,

reptile, bird of prey. The wolves would come. Dark Girl, there are
no noble creatures of this earth. If there were lions to be found,

they would be lean, flesh hungry. You did not come to this world
dewy, translucent with newness; you were a kick, a shriek,

a clawing in the gut to be let out. I am charged to guide you—
show you sign for hunger, symbol for teeth. There will be

lessons in camouflage and stillness. Lessons of the switchgrass
and the snakes therein. There will be lessons for the blood,

a lesson for the fire. Signs for stay and go. A circling: the way
we hold you now—and the raptors overhead, descending.

Along the Way to Dockery Farms

It was the Christmas the brother killed himself & she was crying into my shirt & someone (I can't remember who) said: *everything will be all right; one day it will be better* & I said: *No, no* & I said: *you will never forget & there was never a time when you were happy without a darkness lurking & you & he were powerless to stop it & there was nothing you could do* & I could not fix my mouth to say how I came to this knowing because every heart has its solstice & its ache is unrelenting.

In the Years Following Rescue

I was drowning. I had been drowning all my life
when he found me in this place and I was saved.

I loved the river and the river loved me.
I was dying of such love. Do you know, I asked,

of the world underwater? How the words come slow
as if from great distance? Where I am from

there is neither sky nor stars. I said this as we were
sitting by the river. Here, he said. This is the wreck

where you were found. When you were lifted from its ruin,
the words fled your mouth like hummingbirds,

golden in the falling sun, hovering a moment
before retreating again into darkness. Here, he said,

when you were listless and learning breath, you reached
to me as if to say, *I want to live.*
                                    And I did, I said. I did.

Then I bent down, and reached out my hand to stir the water.

three

What I Did in My Time Away from Words

Much laundry was done, and much accounting.
Days were spent watching the customs of the trees.
At night the trees wandered down to the river beds
to mingle their slender branches and by morning
were returned again to their appointed places.
I tried to tell others about these nightly assignations,
but they looked at me askance, shook their lovely
heads. They told me the world simply cannot
be that mysterious. I was told that all that could be
known is known and my insistence on this interior
life, for trees or myself, is folly. I fell silent.
But last night, I heard the shuffling of roots.
I ran outside to find the fields emptied again,
and an apple sapling leaning on my sidewalk.
I looked away only a moment and it was gone.

Meridian, MS 1963: My Mother Considers the Mechanics of Flight

I want to save you, dark girl of thunderhead, dark girl falling upward.
I want to tell you the voices fluttering in the dark of your body are all true:

you will leave this place, and those who would harm you will pass over.
    Dark Girl,
even now you cannot be held within your soft, slight bones—synapses

firing all at once—first the aura, then borealis of red and yellow light
sparking your firmament—your body thundering, writhing, thundering

against the ground. What did you find in those liminal places? Consider
the jewel-throated hummingbird; keep your wings by beating them faster

than the human eye can see. Did your mother stand guard,
gently thrust a stick into your mouth to hold the tongue, to save it?

I Begin My Confession

For the record, I did nothing unseemly.
When you hungered, I fed you and
when you thirsted, I gave you drink.

But I did not watch you wither
without satisfaction, which is to say
I may have sinned. I waited

for a compassion to descend
like a gentle rain from angels,
but the more I prayed (oh, I prayed)

the cancer marched onward, the jaw
then at last the tongue, so you grunted
every need. At night sometimes,

you let out a gurgling sound
like you were choking on yourself
and I got up, gathered your body

and wiped your face. I'm not sure
if I prayed for you or myself,
but I let you live, if only because

I knew you suffered. Shouldn't I
be ashamed of myself? Shouldn't I?

The Burgomaster Said I Could Do Whatever I Wanted to You

Then added: *I will turn my back and look away.*
But as you entered into the room, shuffling and
jangling your chains and smelling of day after day
after day of yourself, I thought of forgiveness.
Which is to say: I thought of myself. I stood
without a word to offer. Then I remembered fire,
the fires we fled, the night after day after night
in darkness, and the girl's screams in her dying,
the baby you left on the grass, crying and crying
until it didn't. Then the growling of the dogs.
All the while, you were silent and watching me
as you had always been. And as I turned to leave,
I thought to myself: *I can look away. I can choose
to give you nothing. I can save myself, save myself.*

Theodore Bilbo and I Begin Our Crossing

We rowed farther and farther out
onto that river when a great fog

descended upon us so that we could see
neither the shore we left nor the shore ahead;

we could not even sense our direction
against the current. So we picked a direction,

then another, then another and rowed furiously,
but we found the rowing felt endless,

we were lost and the river was without dimension.
The fog thickened still and as night fell,

suddenly light appeared, then appeared
all around us and then, there were voices,

We called out to them but they would not
answer; we rowed toward them, but they

could not be found. But the river became crowded
with these travelers, with the deafening concert

of that calling, calling, and calling with voices
which if they had arms could still not reach.

How the Past Tense Turns a Whole Sentence Dark

Somewhere, it is night—a night in which you still love me.
If you asked—*how long must suffering last*—I would say

you loved me once and lead you forward along the hedgerows.
Ahead, the night where you loved me is a room in space.

Curtains drawn. Its door closed to us. Inside, my head above
your heart. Your legs between or over mine. The silence we kept.

How I would open my mouth to break it, and you would
shake your head, as if to say *no words* and turn my body to fill it.

It is night. We are outside ourselves, mouths filling with dark
cinnamon smoke, outside the house of past tense. Inside, those bodies

do not belong to us. Inside, they will love unceasingly. When
we are dead, the angels will gather, throw open the door, call out

to the night: *where shall they find rest?* Even the stars will be
ashamed of us, point their fiery arms in all directions.

Everything Men Know about Women

The ream of empty pages bound into
Everything Men Know about Women

was the joke, of course. And we laughed
because we were young then and

certain the pages could bear the filling.
But now. These years later, I say

I was there, I was there when you wrote
that first thing you learned. You ask me,

Do you remember what it was? Your face
grows dark with forgetting and you reach for

your glass. We are twenty years gone
in this smoky bar and you ask, *How long*

have I known you? I am warm with drink
and say, *It is nice to be known.* My mouth

grows heavy with all the things left unsaid
between friends, so I say: *I am very happy*

to fill the silence. You flag the bartender,
order another (your last, like the last one),

look me in the eye and ask: *Are you?* I reach
for your hand then: *Just now. I am happy now.*

This is the last true thing I say to you.

The Peonies at the Bodega

Were this a poem, and I were just arranging the sound,
we would be standing in *rain* and not *snow*.

I would have left on foot and gathered my coat against weather;
I would not hail a taxi. I would not raise my hand against

the glass as if to gesture against mourning. You would not be left
standing alone among the hothouse flowers at the bodega

near Mott and Broome. When we made love that afternoon,
we would have taken all our clothes off. You would have

removed your left sock, for example. In the poem I would write,
the women on the street would not have noticed how much we loved

or that we fairly glowed with it. Nor would they bustle by—
    cluck-clucking,
smiling knowingly. In the poem, you would have hailed the cab yourself,

opened the door, shut me up in it. I would have kept my eyes forward.
I would not have watched you grow smaller and smaller through

the rear window. You would not have waved and waved and waved.
In the poem, it would be near dusk; there would be a metaphor

about how the earth participates in the end of things. I'd mention
the owners of the bodega were an old married couple, restocking

the produce to guard against decay. I'd mention the flowers;
they would be peonies. Peonies would stand in for something else.

Consolation

I wanted to call when I heard he left in the night without warning.
I would have told how he woke me once at three in the morning

and whispered: *it is snowing* and led me into the wind to dance,
snow swirling up from the hem of my robe until snow was all around us

and overhead. And I would tell you we invited the weather inside,
and the cold gathered, great drifts of snow gathering in the halls

until it became unbearable. That it was unbearable he knew,
just as he knew he was the cause of it. And in the years it takes

to clear the ice floes from your kitchen, you will come to know
this leaving is for the best, that there are new summers, kinder latitudes.

We Are Soldiers in the Army of the Lord

The old gods are falling. So are we all.
Citizen, they will not tell you that falling

can be forward motion, or that freedom is less
being broken than will to rise. Go, my dark sweet girl.

Praise our fresh dead. Raise them up—
Call each by rightful name.

Citizen. Citizen.

Have they called you animal, Citizen?
You are bone and spirit too.

Rise, girl, for we are soldiers.
This earth is littered with our fallen.

Weep not. The ground shifts
with the ghosts of the fallen. Rise.

Theodore Bilbo & I Consider the End of Days

The world we knew has fallen,
its head lolling like the dying
sunflowers of the field—

it retires after its long day &
leaves Teddy & me alone
& drunk on the veranda.

We'll drink all night,
& no one will care
where we have gone.

Under the stars & fireflies
we'll twine our limbs
until all their light blurs into

one great weight upon us
& we'll finally untwine from
this patch of earth. He'll be

just drunk enough to apologize,
say: *There was the war.*
Remember? We lost & I'll say:

There was war, & a war, then
another & another & the wind will pool
in the swelling distance between us

& he'll grope for a word
suspended in the dark. *Abandon.*
I'll say. *I abandoned you.*

It could neither go on nor last.
We'll embrace—my arms around
his back and I'll feel something

like his heart knocking
against my opened hand &
I can't say that I won't love him

then as now, nor that I haven't
loved him like I love myself.
I couldn't stay, Teddy, I'll say.

I had to live & he'll watch the hills
& the cotton will pace the distance &
he'll take in the still air &

he won't look me in the eye after that.
We will grieve. Our grief will blot
the light left in the surrounding night &

the wisteria blooms will roll like
the many eyes of our dead.
We will grieve. We will be done with it.

And through the Dark

a calm descends. The granite rises
thirty feet. And through the rock,
a stream breaks then flows,

reaches out unbroken to the ground.
And beyond is where the field sprawls
bearing hay bales harvested.

The doors to the barn
were left open. The horses stand

abandoned and listless
in the pasture. The long-lashed
foals attend our passing.

You asked: *where are we going?*
Back and back again, I said
and folded my fingers tight
between yours, and drove until

there was neither car nor skin-sack,
only light—yellowing, honey-thick.

We were the car and road, granite
and stream. The pasture and foal.

The barn door and gate.
We were the darkness you feared.

We were light, our own undoing.

We would have choked
if we still breathed.

Theodore Bilbo and I Take Tea on the Veranda

The afternoon, even we had to admit, grew more majestic as it went. It was the kind of day toward the end of winter that reminded you that even winter could relent. So we took our tea outside, although it was probably still too cold for it. Quite out of order, I said: *I cannot be this angry for so long. It's become exhausting.* You looked back at me steady and unsurprised and blew your tea which let off a little steam into the air. *I owe a great deal of apologies*, you said, *but none to you. What have I done to you but be a disappointment?* And from where I sat, the sun began to fall in a blinding way, so that at once you disappeared and became shadow. *One day*, you said, *someone will speak of us and say we had an understanding, which is not the same thing as agreeing.* I stirred the tea, and nodded. But that's not what I meant. Not what I meant at all.

The Living Always Chase the Dead

Even the ghosts grow distant and file out.
This town, this looted house, this cracked foundation.
This is the last of all our summers. There are few
monuments. The citizens, they take them. There will be
no monuments when we are gone. The house on the other corner:
that woman is dead. Her sons are dead. There was a war here,
and then another; the battledead still wrestling in the underbrush.

If you ask, *Where am I? How do I return?*—
the citizens are friendly; they still give directions relative to
where things used to be. Stand before the everlasting fires of Zion
and remember yourself. The boys in the swamp are dead.
The men who killed the boys in the swamp, too, and when
we put up markers, the citizens bear them away. The plum
tree is fruiting; the oak still making a mess of the sidewalk.
If you are still, you could mistake the dead in the underbrush for wind.

four

Okatibbee River 2012

Sudden brightness
         then thunderclap

Dark Girl,

the world comes all at once

like the Red Sea
regaining its contours

after miracle

On Bathing Her Mother

How easy to imagine you dead, now that I am older,
watching you bathe your mother, watching her raise her hand to you.

Watching you catalog all the ways she's raised her hand to you.
You've memorized the gesture. How like a child she is—

this hand is an offering as she extends one arm. Her palm is cupped and
    empty.
She extends the other. Later, you swear I won't have to do this.

'This'?, I ask. *This falling apart*, you said. *You watching me fall apart.*
But there is only me and you. It could only be this way because daughters

need the bodies of our mothers to know time and its measure. Otherwise,
I'm just a body flung in space. It could only be us in this dim lit room,

water running over, my fingers in your hair, tracing the figure your body
    makes,
our shadows tangled, indistinguishable—my hands retracing you as
    the light falls.

Theodore Bilbo and I Survey the Ruin

We have been parties to a magnificent wreck,
but all I know now (My God, it has been so long)

is open sea and I am adrift in it. So many suns and
moons and constellations have passed overhead;

I have forgotten myself. What I remember is my making—
the falling, the flight. Weightlessness then consequence.

Then you joined me and we rejoiced. But after
so many suns and moons, so many days spent

circling the water, the long days and nights with
neither bearing nor wind, we turn from one another—

hands clasped, back to back. You measure day
and I, the night. The nights are so much longer now.

I measure the distance from star to star and I have
begun renaming them, each for a different form of misery.

Panic. Idleness. Cold. When I run out of words,
I make them up. I mouth a name for the resentment

reserved only for those closest to you, and the shame
one feels in need. A name for the slow fragrant

bloom of love to loathing. Coincidentally, that name
echoes my own. But tonight, I have finished

my work—the stars so bright and close, and
my misery no longer any use. It remains:

you are not water for drinking. You are not shore.
It remains: we are adrift and we will waste away.

My Grandfather Appears to Me on the Eve of
My Grandmother's Passing

Build this house, he said.
Even then, I knew it was night

and I was dreaming,
that this was metaphor—

the hammer in his hand,
the ladder I was holding
and his descending.

I wanted to say no,
this house does not belong to us,
nothing belongs to us
anymore,

the cupboard is bare and
any message we send
will return.

I know this is a dream, I said.
I know I am dreaming.

But this did not stop my rise into
what can only be described as
a radiance, an intersection

between all that is living and
all that has lived. And because
what is living is weak

and it is the living who haunt the dead—
I woke, speechless and wanting.

This Is How I Love Her

I can't do it all at once, but when I do
I must start small, that photograph
by the window. She was a child then;
I must remember she came to this earth
whole before it broke her more thoroughly
than most. Then, the apologies come:
I am sorry, so sorry for the leaving.
We are born here, grow older, then leave.
This could not be helped. But now,
I love her as one loves a child, all risk
but in reverse. When someone speaks my name,
she sighs plaintively and says: *Oh look,*
look what I've done to Emily as if this were
a kind of confession. Here is my great forgiving.
She was so young, so young. Perhaps I could not
have done better. This is how I love her,
my mother, her mother, the mother of her mother,
our accumulated mistakes and misgivings.

After Forty Days, Go Marry Again

She was only just here. That's her,
that's her in the red dress, that's
her, too, fists full of balloons as if
she would fly away. That's her at the
bottom of the hill. She ran as fast as she
could toward the top, arms wide,
cheeks flushed. She reached me
breathless and toppled both of us.
That's her, and her again,
her black hair in pigtails held
in yellow ball-stay barrettes.
Girls of that age are particular
about such things. I sleep in her room
some nights with all the lights on,
everything as she left it.

There she is in Biloxi, there she is
and there she is and there she is.
There she is: bits of black hair
and the earrings. They say: *maybe
that's not her.* Look. There.
The ball-stay barrettes. Yellow,
flowers stretched around. There she
is at Christmas. There she is that
summer she grew three inches. They say:
after forty days, go marry again. But
there she is, and there she is again with

her friend from class. That girl is dead too.
There she is at the carnival. There she is.
Her fists clenched on the balloons. There
she is at the door, lunchbox in one hand,
waving with the other. At night,
I pretend to sleep; there she is
standing over me as if there are words
left to say. There she is. There
she is in the dark.

Theodore Bilbo Mistakes Me for the Angel of Death

You must have known the words were poisoned,
after they cancered your mouth,
overtook the lips, a cheek, the jaw—

Even when what was once your face
bloomed ruin, you kept on saying them.
And now, with what is left of your mouth

I think I hear you saying, *please, please*
and I cradle your head in my hand
and lift you to the cup to slake your thirst.

I didn't know until you turned your face from me
that you expected less than mercy or
that I had nothing but mercy left to give.

Kyrie: Notes to the God I Cannot See

When you consider creation, Lord—think of me:
this misfiring body, this broken machine.

We die here on earth, spinning like a child's top—
spin and gyre then falling down. Have mercy.

This may not be of much import, Lord—there is so much
wind and distance. So many birds and stars. There are those

who know not of their suffering. Knowledge of suffering
is amplitude. Lord, have mercy. Is this what is meant

to clothe a man in thunder? I know I suffer, Lord
and I am afraid. Have mercy. Shall I praise this body?

What can I praise when all You have done
may be undone? Have mercy. Have mercy.

The Trouble with Lightning

is it travels without resistance
through any body of water.

The human body is
just another body of water to lightning.

The trouble is that it can miss you entirely,
pace the earth alongside of you and

be drawn up your running legs,
bead off the fingers like pearls.

The trouble is it won't sit in the corner and
wait for you to gather it like a javelin to hoist

in the direction of the deserving.
The trouble is mostly in what a man deserves.

On any given Thursday afternoon,
lightning can find you

sitting in the car on the highway, and
bore through the sky above.

The trouble with lightning is
how rarely it kills a man.

Meridian, MS 1964: They Moaned So Much They Called It Song

and to that music we swayed. And we called the music sweet
and measured our days between our sorrows and joys.

Dark Girl, so great were our joys, we named you for them,
prayed you would live long so that your joy could outweigh

our troubles. Do you remember the night we counted our missing—
how after the house emptied of men, I took you to the back room,

turned on the radio and we danced? Remember how they found
the bodies, stacked like lumber beneath the earthdam? Did you know

I came to you in the night, watched you in your sleep, reached out
to stroke your hair? I went from room to room in the dark—counting

and recounting my children. Dark Girl, those boys were stripped
of their bark, huddled together as if from cold. Outside, the women's cries

bleated against the windows. To say this wasn't joy would be a lie.
You were accounted for, you were held in the walls of this house,

and for that reason, I sat in the chair in the parlor, sang songs of praise,
watched the street from the inside, rocked myself to and fro.

Meridian, MS 1964: At the Solstice, the World Is Flooded
with Light

In the hour of my death, I knew there were places without darkness.
For a time it quartered itself in the hearts of men and in the growing hour,

I learned what a man could do. Did you know most men won't look
    death in the eye,
even if it's not their own? No. In that moment, he will turn away.

A sense of shame will wash over him. He will shift foot to foot,
and cast down his eyes. Something within him will go dark and

he will know his nakedness before God. All that follows is logistics,
a moving of the earth to cover the work of the hands. Did you know

that when you kill a man, you own that body? The body returns to you;
you own even its dust. It is your charge and yours alone to keep it buried.

You must thwart all that would offer aid to the dead—the moon,
    the trees, the night flowers.
The tree frogs: their alarm that is often mistaken for song.

Theodore Bilbo and I Survey the Contours of Zion

It is all so
devastatingly
familiar.

The hills walled
with cypress,
bands of willows and
the sea,

     each glittering drop

rolling unceasingly toward
this new horizon called forever,

the slack-jawed surprise
of the oysters
releasing their pearls

to line each square inch
        of shore.

Be still. Still,
you are standing
    next to me—

No version of
paradise

have we imagined
with the other.

And as we are
already dead,

there is nothing
either of us
can do.

five

At the Repast

When we gathered at the house, while the men all looked at their shoes
and the women whispered, *baby, baby, baby,* she sat down with a fist full
of paper napkins and folded them into birds. When she filled her hands,
she crossed the room to the hearth and threw a bird into the flames, then
another, then another until she had destroyed all she created. Years later
when I asked her what she meant, she couldn't remember. *The worst has
already happened to us,* she said. *What good is metaphor now?*

What We Find at the End of the World

For you, I crossed a great deal of country and stood at the end of the
    world
to grieve, thinking that would be the end of it. But days later, I heard

bare feet padding behind me in the kitchen, or the den. Then you grew
    bolder,
sitting at the end of my bed, waiting as I pretended to sleep in the dark.

I could not speak to you because I was still so very angry. But then,
just the other night I had a dream, less visitation than remembrance—

It was the first day we met, and you cupped my cheek with your open
    hand
and said: *You are so very beautiful.* As I opened my mouth to speak,

you shook your head: *No, it is in the way you've learned to take up space.*
I was saddened and moved by so much honesty at once that I held you

and felt you disappearing in my arms, which I suppose is what happened.
I was so startled that I sat upright in bed and said: *I forgive you,*

although who am I to forgive you when we are all unknowable?
I reached out my hand and then I was alone again in that dark room.

How to Love the Country of Your Birth

Mississippi, place of my greatest sorrow,
raise your hand to me like that again
so that I may kiss it. Grab my throat again

so I can offer the murder of crows roosting there.
Listen, my love, even a crow will stop its caw
when it sees me reaching back for you. Even the crows

will sing in astonishment. They sing of homecoming
as sweetly as any nightingale. The song says, *take me back.*
The song says, *stay.* The song begs you to speak

my full name and say it sweetly. The song
is the same as it's always been: *love me, love me—*
love me back, love me always, love me still.

Theodore Bilbo and I Wander the Farther Shore

From the terrace, we can see the river, you said.
Next time I'll bring my tackle. And you led me out,
pointing to a rockspit below near the water's edge
where the fish swarmed. I looked and looked
until at last I found them—fistfuls of silver rising and falling.
We stood a long time while the sun wearied itself,
and commented on the comings and goings of the barges
on the farther shore, the men filling their pails with fish
as they wandered the riverbanks until it grew too dark
for the watching. But by morning the barges were gone,
the winds had shifted, and there was a taste in the air—
you said sulfur, I said brimstone—as if the earth across the water
had split itself and was consumed in fire while we were sleeping.
Overhead, flocks of dark birds beat the air and let out a sound like loss.
And I said: *Has the earth known all along this sound of leaving,*
waiting until this moment to reveal it to us? And you said:
Where have all the barges gone? Do they seek each their own ocean?
And I said: *Maybe the loons, the loons. The loons.*

How to Grieve

This isn't about particulars—this isn't a story about
the way she cradled a mango in the gully of her hand.

It isn't that she said each fruit bears memory:
this one, the red earth in a rainy season, or
that one, the easy smile of the beloved.

This isn't a story about my aunt in the summer
of the four o'clocks. How she asked me to kill them and
I kept killing them. Or that they refused to die.

This isn't a story about the wife you left, or left you.
It's not even about the leaving. It's about all the places

you can't come back to. Those who leave
and stay gone. The things that never leave.

This pouring rain, for example. You and me in this room
alone and together in grief, for example. These words

I want to offer in comfort. How they fail.
The way ruin rises silently as flood.

The way this body is not a sandbag, but
how I will cover yours with mine.

Like now, my love. Like this.

Theodore Bilbo and I Wait Out the Storm

We were standing under the eaves and you said: *Have you noticed that the world is the same thing over and over? The same miseries, the same cares?*

And I said: *Do you imagine that at the center of the earth there are two people, just like us, wrestling and arguing and that conflict keeps the earth turning and sends the fires from the earth into the ocean?*

And you said: *What if we stopped? Would the earth float away toward ever greater catastrophes?*

And you reached for my hand, and I gave you my hand. This was done with excruciating tenderness and we fell silent and waited for the rain to break.

Theodore Bilbo and I at Last Turn Face to Face

There is a rock-like growth in this body,
fissuring of its own weight as if to remind me

what is dead must escape the body.
That the leaving is often what saved you.

I am older. I can find a bottom to myself
where I once could not. How small I've become

once there is no looking out, left only
with a spiraling inward gaze, left the tasks

of inventory and measure. But there is this:
once there was me and there was you

and from my mouth like a shock of doves
comes forgiveness. Believe me,

I am as surprised as anyone.

Acknowledgments

I gratefully acknowledge the following publications, where some of these poems first appeared (some in different form):

The Bakery—"Meridian, MS 1958: My Grandmother Meditates on the Miracles of the Christ," "Meridian, MS 1964: At the Solstice, the World Is Flooded with Light"
Beloit Poetry Journal—"After Forty Days, Go Marry Again"
Poetry Magazine—"At the Repast"
VQR—"1973: My Mother Cleaves Herself in Two," "Theodore Bilbo Attends My Sickbed"
West Branch—"Meridian, MS 1963: My Mother Considers the Mechanics of Flight"

Many thanks to the Tupelo Press 30/30 project for which many drafts of these poems were first written.

I am grateful for the support of the Colrain Manuscript Conference and the Sewanee Writers' Conference; thanks to Joan Houlihan, Martha Rhodes, Mary Jo Salter, and Danny Anderson.

This book could not have happened without the love and understanding of my family: Mom, Dad, Mitch, John, Manon, and Leen. Or my Nashville extended family: Kendra DeColo, Gary McDowell, Elizabeth Sparger, and Margy Smith Roark.

But as always most special thanks is reserved for those whose love carries me every day: Christina, Chuck, and Marsha. I could not have done this without Christina's keen eye or the Pierce Manor writing room. You have given me so much; I could not love you more.

Other Books in the Crab Orchard Series in Poetry